FOR THE LOVE OF SOCCER!

BY **PELÉ**, THREE-TIME
WORLD CUP CHAMPION

ILLUSTRATED BY
Frank Morrison

LITTLE, BROWN AND COMPANY
New York   Boston

Ever since I was a little boy,
I knew **SOCCER** was the
game for **me.**

I would play with anyone,

anytime,

anywhere!

A few little taps or

one big kick–

I **loved** making the ball
do what I wanted it to do.

But practicing my moves

wasn't **anything**

compared to playing

in a **real** game.

When I was on the field, I was part of **something special**. I was part of the **team**.

The **second**
the starting whistle
blasted, every player
exploded into **action**.

Feet flying
over the turf,
we passed,
dribbled,
dodged.

And once the ball landed
in just the right spot . . .

There were times
when that ball
seemed to hang
in midair

forever,

until...

I've won a lot of games. Winning isn't everything, though—

being a good sport is what really counts.

Some people have called me the best soccer player in the **world**.

But I've **never** played for **fame.**

I play for the **love** of the **game.**

MORE ABOUT PELÉ

Pelé was born on October 23, 1940, in a small town in Brazil. His father, Dondinho, and his mother, Dona Celeste, named him Edson Arantes do Nascimento, but everyone called him Dico. He didn't get the nickname Pelé until he was nine or ten. To this day, he has no idea what "Pelé" means or who gave him the name. In fact, he didn't even like the nickname at first. But for some reason it stuck, so that's how he's known in the world today.

Soccer—or football, as he and people in many countries call it—was a big part of Pelé's life right from the start. His father played professionally until he hurt his knee.

He taught his son everything he knew. Dona Celeste, however, didn't want her boy to become a soccer player. She was afraid he'd hurt himself like his father had. In fact, she never attended one of Pelé's games, because she didn't want to see him get injured!

But Pelé loved the sport too much to give it up, even for his beloved mother.

Pelé grew up in a poor neighborhood. No one had money for soccer equipment. So he and his friends made balls out of old socks stuffed with newspapers. They played barefoot on dusty dirt roads. They formed a team and challenged other teams to matches. Some days they'd play soccer from dawn until dusk.

Pelé thought about soccer all the time. He daydreamed about it during school, even though he knew he'd be punished for not paying attention. He came up with schemes to make money to buy equipment. He collected and sold sports cards of famous soccer players. He shined shoes and boots.

It was a few years later, when he was fifteen, that Pelé was noticed by a famous soccer player named Waldemar de Brito. De Brito was so impressed that he helped Pelé sign up with his first professional team. The team was called Santos, after the town where it played.

Santos was far from Pelé's hometown, and at first he was very homesick. Once he packed his bags to take the train back to his family. But soon Pelé returned to the team. How could he do otherwise? Playing professional soccer was his dream, after all.

It was a dream he lived to the fullest. Pelé played for Santos from 1956 until 1974. During those years he also played on Brazil's National Team, helping them win three World Cups, the sport's top worldwide competition. He retired from Santos in 1974, but in 1975 joined a new team, the New York Cosmos.

Soccer wasn't a popular sport in the United States when Pelé first came to America. But thanks in large part to his amazing skills and personality, it soon gained a following that has grown by leaps and bounds. Today, boys and girls across the country play in leagues, in parks, and in their backyards.

Anyone who ever saw Pelé play knows that he was born to be a soccer player. His passion for the game shone through whenever he took to the field. And even today the magic of soccer, that beautiful game, shows in his wide smile when he dribbles or kicks a ball.

To the children of the world,
especially the children of America,
who received me with open arms when I
played for the New York Cosmos. —Pelé

For my home team: Nia,
Nyree, Tyreek, and Nasir.
Dream big! —F.M.

Text copyright © 2010 by Pelé
Illustrations copyright © 2010 by Frank Morrison

Cover art copyright © 2010 by Frank Morrison. Cover design by David Hastings. Cover copyright © 2010 by Hachette Book Group, Inc.

Little, Brown and Company
Hachette Book Group
1290 Avenue of the Americas, New York, NY 10104
Visit us at LBYR.com

Originally published in hardcover with the title *For the Love of Soccer!* by Disney • Hyperion, an imprint of Disney Book Group, in May 2010
First Trade Paperback Edition: June 2020

Little, Brown and Company is a division of Hachette Book Group, Inc. The Little, Brown name and logo are trademarks of Hachette Book Group, Inc.

The publisher is not responsible for websites (or their content) that are not owned by the publisher.

Library of Congress Control Number for the Hardcover Edition: 2009015890

ISBN 978-1-368-05633-5

Printed in the United States of America

CW

10 9 8 7 6 5 4 3